D0481439

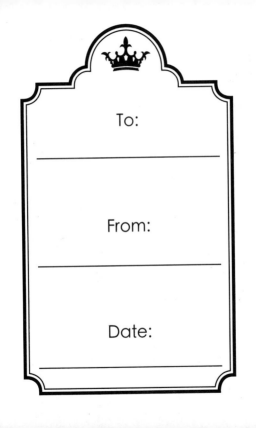

To:

From:

Date:

Keep Calm and Trust God

© 2013   Christian Art Gifts, RSA
            Christian Art Gifts Inc., IL, USA

Designed by Christian Art Gifts

Images used under license from Shutterstock.com

Scripture quotations are taken from the *Holy Bible*, King James Version.
Copyright © 1962 by The Zondervan Corporation. Used by permission.

Scripture quotations are taken from the *Holy Bible*, New Living Translation®, second
edition. Copyright © 1996, 2004 by Tyndale House Publishers, Inc., Carol Stream,
Illinois 60188. All rights reserved.

Scripture quotations are taken from the New King James Version.
Copyright © 1979, 1980, 1982 by Thomas Nelson, Inc. Used by permission.
All rights reserved.

Scripture quotations are taken from the *Holy Bible*, New International Version® NIV®.
Copyright © 1973, 1978, 1984, 2011 by International Bible Society.
Used by permission of Zondervan Publishing House. All rights reserved.

Scripture quotations are taken from the Contemporary English Version®.
Copyright © 1995 by American Bible Society. All rights reserved.

Scripture quotations are taken from the *Holy Bible*, English Standard Version.
Copyright © 2001 by Crossway Bibles, a division of Good News Publishers.
Used by permission. All rights reserved.

Printed in China

ISBN 978-1-4321-0893-9

14   15   16   17   18   19   20   21   22   23   –   12   11   10   9   8   7   6   5   4   3

Keep Calm and Carry On

In late 1939, after the outbreak of World War II, the British Government commissioned a number of morale-boosting posters that would be displayed across the British Isles during the testing times that lay ahead. The first two posters were posted in public places across Britain.

The third and final poster of the set simply read "Keep Calm and Carry On". The plan in place for this poster was to issue it only upon the invasion of Britain by Germany. As this never happened, the poster was never officially seen by the public.

Nearly 60 years later, a bookseller stumbled across a copy hidden amongst a pile of dusty old books bought from an auction. He put the poster up in the store and was amazed at the response.

It is wonderful to think that all these years later, people still find it so appealing and reassuring. And it is even more fitting when we think of how we can trust God and confidently pray even in the most difficult times, knowing that He is with us and will carry us through.

Simply trusting every day;
Trusting through a stormy way;
Even when my faith is small,
Trusting Jesus, that is all.

Trusting as the moments fly,
Trusting as the days go by,
Trusting Him, whate'er befall,
Trusting Jesus, that is all.

Ira Sankey

Faith expects from God what
is beyond all expectation.

Andrew Murray

"Be still, and know
that I am God."

Ps. 46:10

Faith is not believing
that God can, it is
knowing that God will.

Ben Stein

Faith is not belief without proof, but trust without reservation.

Elton Trueblood

Trust in the LORD with all your heart and lean not on your own understanding; in all your ways submit to Him, and He will make your paths straight.

Prov. 3:5-6

Faith is to believe what
we do not see, and the
reward of this faith is
to see what we believe.

St. Augustine

"Blessed are those
who have not seen and
yet have believed."

John 20:29

The beautiful thing about this adventure called faith is that we can count on Him never to lead us astray.

Chuck Swindoll

Fear looks; faith jumps!

Smith Wigglesworth

We fix our eyes not on
what is seen, but on what is
unseen, since what is seen
is temporary, but what is
unseen is eternal.

2 Cor. 4:18

Faith sees the invisible,
believes the unbelievable,
and receives the impossible.

Corrie ten Boom

The LORD is near to all
who call on Him, to all
who call on Him in truth.

Ps. 145:18

All that I have seen teaches
me to trust the Creator
for all I have not seen.

Ralph Waldo Emerson

"I will instruct you and teach
you in the way you should go;
I will counsel you and
watch over you."

Ps. 32:8

The whole being of any
Christian is faith and love.
Faith brings the man to God,
love brings Him to men.

Martin Luther

"I tell you the truth, whoever hears My word and believes Him who sent Me has eternal life and will not be condemned; he has crossed over from death to life."

John 5:24

Faith has to do with
things that are not seen,
and hope with things
that are not in hand.

St. Thomas Aquinas

Faith is being sure of what
we hope for and certain
of what we do not see.

Heb. 11:1

To know God is not
through reason, nor is it
through emotions,
but by faith and love.

A. W. Tozer

A man's heart plans his way,
but the LORD directs his steps.

Prov. 16:9

I believe though I do not
comprehend, and I hold by
faith what I cannot grasp
with the mind.

St. Bernard

This is what the LORD says –
your Redeemer, the Holy One
of Israel: "I am the LORD
your God, who teaches you
what is best for you, who
directs you in the way
you should go."

Isa. 48:17

God's faithfulness means
that God will always do
what He said and fulfill
what He has promised.

Wayne Grudem

Faith is putting all your eggs
in God's basket, then
counting your blessings
before they hatch.

Ramona Carroll

The LORD directs the steps
of the godly. He delights in
every detail of their lives.

Ps. 37:23

Only he who believes is obedient, and only he who is obedient believes.

Dietrich Bonhoeffer

He will not allow your foot
to be moved, He that keeps
you will not slumber.

Ps. 121:3

Every tomorrow has two handles. We can take hold of it with the handle of anxiety, or with the handle of faith.

Henry Ward Beecher

Your word is a lamp
to guide my feet and
a light for my path.

Ps. 119:105

Faith is that strengthening
power within, urging me
on my way, teaching
me all that I must know,
helping to obey. Faith is that
strengthening power within,
lighting the road I trod,
helping me know which
way to go, pointing
the way to God.

Anonymous

Without guidance from God
law and order disappear,
but God blesses everyone
who obeys His Law.

Prov. 29:18

Faith is the victory!
Faith is the victory!
Oh, glorious victory,
That overcomes the world.

John H. Yates

I praise You, LORD,
for being my guide.
Even in the darkest night,
Your teachings fill my mind.

Ps. 16:7

Obedience is the fruit
of faith; patience
the bloom on the fruit.

Christina Rossetti

"But seek ye first
the kingdom of God,
and His righteousness;
and all these things shall
be added unto you."

Matt. 6:33

Do you sometimes think,
if I could just see Christ.
If I could meet Him. If I could
talk to Him personally, then
this life would be easier.
But you have seen Him.
You have met Him. You have
talked to Him personally.
This knowledge, believed in
faith, can make life easier.

Anonymous

41

"You will seek Me and
find Me, when you search
for Me with all your heart."

Jer. 29:13

Faith is to prayer what
the feather is to the arrow;
without faith it will not
hit the mark.

J. C. Ryle

"Take diligent heed to do
the commandment and the
law, which Moses the servant
of the LORD charged you,
to love the LORD your
God, and to walk in all
His ways, and to keep His
commandments, and to
cleave unto Him, and to serve
Him with all your heart
and with all your soul."

Josh. 22:5

44

Following Jesus from day
to day, gently He leads me
along the way; e'er will I trust
Him all foes despite,
by faith and not by sight.

Clara M. Brooks

Take delight in the LORD,
and He will give you the
desires of your heart.

Ps. 37:4

Faith is the highest passion
in a human being. Many in
every generation may not
come that far, but none
comes further.

Søren Kierkegaard

Be still before the LORD
and wait patiently for Him.

Ps. 37:7

That's the thing about faith.
If you don't have it you can't
understand it. And if you do,
no explanation is necessary.

Kira Nerys

Seek the LORD and
His strength, seek
His face continually.

1 Chron. 16:11

Reason is an action of
the mind; knowledge is a
possession of the mind;
but faith is an attitude of the
person. It means you are
prepared to stake yourself
on something being so.

Michael Ramsey

"Your ears shall hear a word
behind you, saying,
'This is the way, walk in it,'
when you turn to the right
or when you turn to the left."

Isa. 30:21

I've learned to walk by faith,
not by sight. God's leadings
don't have to make sense.
Some of the wisest direction
I've received has been
ridiculous from a human
viewpoint. So if God tells you
to write someone, write.
If He tells you to serve
somewhere, serve.
Trust Him and take the risk.

Bill Hybels

53

This God is our God
for ever and ever:
He will be our guide
even unto death.

Ps. 48:14

Bestow upon me also,
O Lord my God,
understanding to know You,
diligence to seek You,
wisdom to find You, and
a faithfulness that may
finally embrace You.

Thomas Aquinas

He guides the humble
in what is right and
teaches them His way.

Ps. 25:9

Reason saw not,
till faith sprung the light.

John Dryden

Whoever believes
in the Son has eternal life.

John 3:36

There are many things that are essential to arriving at true peace of mind, and one of the most important is faith, which cannot be acquired without prayer.

John Wooden

You guide me with Your
counsel, and afterward You
will receive me to glory.

Ps. 73:24

Faithfulness and truth
are the most sacred
excellencies and
endowments of the
human mind.

Cicero

"If you listen to Me,
you will be safe and secure
without fear of disaster."

Prov. 1:33

At the beginning of every act of faith, there is often a seed of fear. For great acts of faith are seldom born out of calm calculation.

Max Lucado

I know, LORD, that we humans are not in control of our own lives.

Jer. 10:23

Faith is the master, and
reason the maid-servant.

Martin Luther

The LORD will guide you
continually, and satisfy your
needs in parched places,
and make your bones
strong, and you shall be like
a watered garden, like
a spring of water, whose
waters never fail.

Isa. 58:11

He that takes truth
for his guide, and duty
for his end, may safely
trust to God's providence
to lead him aright.

Blaise Pascal

"Call to Me and I will answer
you, and I will tell you great
and mighty things,
which you do not know."

Jer. 33:3

Faith is a living, daring
confidence in God's grace,
so sure and certain that a
man could stake his life
on it a thousand times.

Martin Luther

If any of you lacks wisdom,
let him ask God, who gives
generously to all without
reproach, and it will
be given him.

James 1:5

The faithful person lives
constantly with God.

Clement of Alexandria

"So I say to you:
Ask and it will be given
to you; seek and you will find;
knock and the door will
be opened to you. For
everyone who asks receives;
the one who seeks finds;
and to the one who knocks,
the door will be opened."

Luke 11:9-10

Thus says the LORD, your Redeemer, the Holy One of Israel: "I am the LORD your God, who teaches you to profit, who leads you in the way you should go."

Isa. 48:17

Weave in faith and
God will find the thread.

Proverb

"It is God who is at work in you, both to will and to work for His good pleasure."

Phil. 2:13

Faith is the vision of the heart;
it sees God in the dark
as well as in the day.

Anonymous

When Jesus spoke again to
the people, He said,
"I am the light of the world.
Whoever follows Me will never
walk in darkness, but will
have the light of life."

John 8:12

"Everything is possible
for one who believes."

Mark 9:23

Faith makes all things
possible ... love makes
all things easy.

Dwight L. Moody

The greatest faith of all, and
the most effective, is to live
day by day trusting Him.
It is trusting Him so much that
we look at every problem
as an opportunity to see
His work in our life.

Rick Joyner

God gave us a spirit not
of fear but of power
and love and self-control.

2 Tim. 1:7

How often does God ask us to step into the water before He will part it? Many times that's all He is waiting for – for you and me to get our feet wet.

Bonnie Ricks

God saved us and called us
to live a holy life. He did this,
not because we deserved
it, but because that was
His plan from before the
beginning of time – to show us
His grace through Christ Jesus.

2 Tim. 1:9

Justifying faith implies, not only a divine evidence or conviction that God was in Christ, reconciling the world unto Himself, but a sure trust and confidence that Christ died for my sins, that He loved me and gave Himself for me.

John Wesley

Out of suffering comes the
serious mind; out of salvation,
the grateful heart; out of
endurance, fortitude; out
of deliverance, faith.

John Ruskin

God is able to bless you abundantly, so that in all things at all times, having all that you need, you will abound in every good work.

2 Cor. 9:8

Faith is a reasoning trust,
a trust which reckons
thoughtfully and
confidently upon the
trustworthiness of God.

John R. Stott

Faith is: dead to doubts,
dumb to discouragements,
blind to impossibilities.

Anonymous

I can do everything through Christ, who gives me strength.

Phil. 4:13

Faith is taking the first step
even when you don't
see the whole staircase.

Martin Luther King, Jr.

Faith is believing He, the
miracle worker, can turn my
stone-cold indifference
into a fire of love toward
certain "unlovables."

Pamela Reeve

The smallest seed of faith is
better than the largest
fruit of happiness.

Henry David Thoreau

You, LORD God, are my
mighty rock and my
fortress. Lead me and
guide me, so that Your
name will be honored.

Ps. 31:3

When a train goes through a tunnel and it gets dark, you don't throw away the ticket and jump off. You sit still and trust the engineer.

Corrie ten Boom

My God shall supply all your
need according to His riches
in glory by Christ Jesus.

Phil. 4:19

I do not want merely to possess a faith, I want a faith that possesses me.

Charles Kingsley

Since we have been justified
through faith, we have
peace with God through
our Lord Jesus Christ.

Rom. 5:1

Worry ends
where faith begins.

George Müller

The gift of faith no limit knows,
Save God's unbounded Word;
It triumphs o'er its giant foes,
And glorifies the blessed Lord.

Daniel S. Warner

Faith is deliberate confidence
in the character of God
whose ways you may not
understand at the time.

Oswald Chambers

Seek not to understand
that you may believe,
but believe that you
may understand.

St. Augustine

You will show the right path
to all who worship You.

Ps. 25:12

Faith and works are bound up in the same bundle. He that obeys God trusts God; and he that trusts God obeys God. He that is without faith is without works; and he that is without works is without faith.

Charles H. Spurgeon

We live by faith, not by sight.

2 Cor. 5:7

Faith grows from
little seeds of love.

Anonymous

Faith is like electricity.
You can't see it,
but you can see the light.

Anonymous

"Your faith has saved you.
Go in peace."

Luke 7:50

God never made a promise
that was too good to be true.

Dwight L. Moody

"I have prayed for you that
your faith may not fail."

Luke 22:32

If you desire faith, then you
have faith enough.

Elizabeth Barrett Browning

"Don't be afraid;
just believe."

Mark 5:36

The army of Israel looked at Goliath through the eyes of man and said he's too big to beat. David looked at him through the eyes of God and said he's too big to miss.

Wally Carter

The work of God is this:
to believe in
the One He has sent.

John 6:29

Faith expects from God what
is beyond all expectation.

Andrew Murray

Reason is the greatest
enemy that faith has.

Martin Luther

If faith produce no works,
I see that faith is not a living
tree. Thus faith and works
together grow, no separate
life they never can know.
They're soul and body, hand
and heart, what God hath
joined, let no man part.

Hannah Moore

A person consists of
his faith. Whatever is
his faith, even so is he.

Proverb

Make every effort to add to your faith goodness; and to goodness, knowledge; and to knowledge, self-control; and to self-control, perseverance; and to perseverance, godliness; and to godliness, brotherly kindness; and to brotherly kindness, love.

2 Pet. 1:5-7

God always gives His best
to those who leave the
choice with Him.

Jim Elliot

Faith is the foundation of all society. We have only to look around and see this.

Dwight L. Moody

It is by grace you have been
saved, through faith – and
this not from yourselves,
it is the gift of God.

Eph. 2:8

"Anyone who believes
in Me will live."

John 11:25

God has not called me
to be successful; He has
called me to be faithful.

Mother Teresa

Be faithful until death, and I will give you the crown of life.

Rev. 2:10

The faithful love of the LORD never ends! His mercies never cease. Great is His faithfulness; His mercies begin afresh each morning.

Lam. 3:22-23

Memory keeps gratitude
fresh and gratitude
keeps faith fruitful.

Dale Ralph Davis

See that your faith bringeth
forth obedience, and
God in due time will cause
it to bring forth peace.

John Owen

The only thing that counts
is faith expressing
itself through love.

Gal. 5:6